I0750269

FINISHING LINE PRESS
www.finishinglinepress.com

Pandemic Lent
A Season in Poems

poems by

Jayne Moore Waldrop

Finishing Line Press
Georgetown, Kentucky

Pandemic Lent
A Season in Poems

ISBN 978-1-64662-486-7 First Edition

ACKNOWLEDGMENTS

"What I've Learned in a Pandemic" appeared in *In Isolation: An Anthology* (Alternative Field Notes 2020).

Publisher: Leah Huete de Maines
Editor: Christen Kincaid
Cover Art: : John C.T. Waldrop
Author Photo: Tim Webb
Cover Design: Elizabeth Maines McCleavy

Order online: www.finishinglinepress.com
also available on amazon.com

Author inquiries and mail orders:
Finishing Line Press
P. O. Box 1626
Georgetown, Kentucky 40324
U. S. A.

Table of Contents

Lenten Haiku.. 1

What I've Learned in a Pandemic 48

In loving memory
LaVerne Mitchell Waldrop
1953-2020

Preface

On the Christian calendar Lent is a forty-day period of self-examination, prayer, and fasting that imitates the time Jesus spent in the wilderness. It's the season to prepare for Easter, the celebration of Christ's resurrection.

Instead of giving up something for Lent this year, I took a different path, one inspired by Brother Paul Quenon's recent book, *In Praise of the Useless Life: A Monk's Memoir* (Ave Maria Press 2018). Since 1958 Br. Paul has lived as a Trappist monk at the Abbey of Gethsemani in rural central Kentucky. He entered the monastery when Thomas Merton, or Father Louis as he was known within the order, served as novice master. Merton guided the novices in their first steps toward monastic life.

Br. Paul's memoir describes his cloistered and disciplined life as one filled with prayer, work, music, nature, and poetry. He's especially fond of the poems of Emily Dickinson. He describes Dickinson, a well-known recluse who kept to her own home and garden, as a soul sister who "often thinks and sounds like a monk." Br. Paul writes that Dickinson's chosen "narrowing of living space seemed to expand the circumference of her mind and heart."

In his daily prayer and meditation, Br. Paul often incorporates haiku writing as "an articulation of the gift of that moment, a brief conclusion to the time spent in silence. Being short, the haiku will not become just another distraction." His haiku stay close to nature, a constant in his spiritual life as well as in the traditional Japanese poetry style.

For the 2020 Lenten season, I adopted Br. Paul's habit of writing haiku as a commitment to find stillness and awareness of the world around me. Surely, I thought, I can put together a haiku—seventeen syllables—each day during Lent to capture "the gift of that moment." Little did I know how life would change during these forty days and how I would experience my own "narrowing of living space."

These short poems—one a day, sometimes more as awareness or anxiety grew—move from the usual somber mood of Ash Wednesday (February 26) to an angst-filled acceleration of the COVID-19 pandemic by Easter (April 12). We sheltered at home as confirmed cases, hospitalizations, and unemployment rates soared. Schools, churches and businesses closed. We wanted news of a cure or vaccine in response to an invisible threat from the natural world.

Circumstances in our family heightened the unease: A physician niece working on the frontline of the New York City outbreak, surrounded by death and uncertain if protective equipment supplies would last; a dear family member facing a new, unexpected diagnosis of Stage 4 pancreatic cancer; a devastating tornado that roared through Nashville, Tennessee where friends and family live; our son's move home when his university closed its campus and switched to online classes, and my own necessary corrective procedure for blurry vision from a complication of recent eye surgery. The simple daily practice of writing helped me manage a turbulent period I didn't see coming on Ash Wednesday.

As a layperson in both theology and epidemiology, I claim no expertise in either field. My viewpoint has been quite ordinary during this season. The extraordinary stories from the pandemic come from essential workers like those testing and treating the sick, feeding the hungry, delivering the mail and other supplies, sanitizing the grocery store, or checking out customers at the pharmacy. Thank you for serving us, keeping us safe, and saving lives in a time of great need.

April 15, 2020

February 26, 2020
Ash Wednesday

Foreheads delivered—
smooth, furrowed, cold, warm, all shades—
returning to dust.

February 27, 2020

White snow, black ice, cold.
We look for truth in this life
like birds searching seeds.

February 28, 2020

Cold blue skies pull me
from a night spent studying
how much could go wrong.

February 29, 2020

Life leaps past darkness—
accelerates toward light, love,
our mortality.

March 1, 2020

Eyes and heart open
to nature as it was made,
full of care and hope.

March 2, 2020

Today's chilly rain,
more welcome than usual,
waters seeds just sown.

March 3, 2020

Life transforms in an
instant, delivered on winds
or with doctor's words.

March 4, 2020

Whiplash or punch drunk?
Hard to tell the difference
but surely concussed.

March 5, 2020

Hard to be hopeful
when frightened. Could that be faith?
Keep looking for light.

March 6, 2020

Of all my senses
sight surely is favorite.
Please, I need to see.

Right eye recovers—
left in two weeks. First local
COVID case confirmed.

Kentucky declares
state of emergency, starts
scouting for supplies.

March 7, 2020

A few eye floaters,
to be expected, they say.
Working out some bugs.

March 8, 2020

Sunday brunch with friends.
Mediterranean theme
with a round of hugs.

Late-in-the-day light
leads me to find daffodils
blooming. Spring forward.

March 9, 2020

Days like this remind
how fragile we are, the ground
so close to the nose.

March 10, 2020

Sunday brunch host calls—
now sick with fever and cough.
We start counting days.

Conferences cancel,
trip to Mexico called off.
This train's building speed.

We gather each day
at five to hear from Andy,
a new fireside chat.

Governor Andy
confirms more cases, calms, brings
order from chaos.

March 11, 2020

Incubation runs
one to fourteen days, symptoms
appear around fifth.

A sore throat begins.
Allergies, I say, nervous.
A Claritin helps.

Host texts—her husband
now sick. She worries for us
because of our age.

She calls the hotline.
No travel abroad, no known
exposure. No test.

Her voice sounds alarmed
that she's exposed us. Don't worry,
I say, worriedly.

March 12, 2020

Iran's long mass graves
seen from outer space, filling
each day with more dust.

March 13, 2020

Hard to find stillness
with the world coming apart.
I try to sit still.

No symptoms for us—
still no test for our host friend.
Was this bullet dodged?

March 14, 2020

Sleeping with windows
cracked means waking to birdsong
with earliest light.

We social distance
hoping to flatten the curve.
Who knows what comes next?

March 15, 2020

First virtual church—
prayers for peace and a path
through new wilderness.

March 16, 2020

The goal is stillness.
Now a standstill is coming.
We're all sitting still.

Governor reports
Kentucky's first COVID death.
The killer arrives.

"We will get through this
together," Andy tells us.
Stay #HealthyAtHome.

March 17, 2020

We see life transform
before our eyes. May we all
love our small world large.

March 18, 2020

Empty: Streets. Shops. Planes.
Movies. Museums. Barbers.
Diners. Bellies. Lives.

Overloaded: Labs.
Doctors. Nurses. Janitors.
ICUs. Vents. Morgues.

March 19, 2020

Today's rain is warm
but nothing controls my chill.
We shiver alone.

An elder sees her
dead sisters on the sofa,
waiting to escort.

March 20, 2020

My hands are clean, chapped
from repeated washing, fear
of seen and unseen.

Campus closes, son
moves home for college remote.
Empty nest refills.

Like flowers we are—
beautiful, fragile, pushing
our way to the sun.

March 21, 2020

Worry on worry.
No masks, Stage IV, Clorox wafts.
I can't not worry.

March 22, 2020

We road trip to see
bursting pink cherry blossoms
planted near the dead.

March 23, 2020

Gray skies, endless rain
compound the despair I feel
shut inside each day.

March 24, 2020

The kindest offer—
PPE for Greer, gratis—
from one barely known.

March 25, 2020

I wake up worried
but thankful my lungs still breathe,
then wonder how long.

They want us to die
for the Dow, to bow down for
their markets. Hell, no.

March 26, 2020

Wilderness finds us,
grows over us like green moss
on granite headstones.

March 27, 2020

Will we kick and scream
or be the hero, priest-like,
when air will not come?

Some are bound to lose.
We wonder who will lose this
viral roulette game.

Feeling the need to
stitch face masks for family
as a sign of love.

Sewing machine found,
dusted off, bobbin threaded,
recalling old skills.

March 28, 2020

We know masks save us.
We learn early to never
leave home without one.

The world is still so
beautiful—blue skies—spring green—
white, yellow, pink buds.

If these are last days
how do we want to spend them?
Fighting on Facebook?

March 29, 2020

Nature doesn't stop.
Creeks and waterfalls still flow
along sycamores.

Wildflowers still bloom
beside the paths even though
no one walks or sees.

Moss grows thick on stone
surfaces, glistening with
clean, pure, safe droplets.

March 30, 2020

Walking keeps me sane.
I keep distance, but hug up
to trees in full bloom.

Crabapple trees draw
bees and humans still able
to smell spring flowers.

Life pares down to bare
necessities: Breath. Food. Love.
A pod for shelter.

The superficial
falls away. We're left with what
we are, what is real.

Failed president talks
about ratings. Disgust grows
exponentially.

March 31, 2020

They say this death is
like drowning, each breath a fight
for air and for life.

Viral nightmare wakes
me, as I watch family
slip beneath water.

Toddler disappears
through thin ice, teenager dives
in, then husband. Gone.

Along river's edge
I cry while beloveds drown
en masse yet alone.

April 1, 2020

Everything is fine.
We've got this under control.
Happy April Fools.

Loss of touch may be
the hardest part for humans.
We're social primates.

My hands miss my face.
They want to touch, rub, maybe
even pick my nose.

Disinfection is
my new expression of love.
I'd prefer a hug.

As I pass walking,
one house smells like tree blossoms,
another like bleach.

April 2, 2020

Parks and woods and creeks
close, forcing us to circle
asphalt cul de sacs.

45 calls it
China virus but it feels
like Russian roulette.

Each grocery run
forces our dear ones to play
a game of roulette.

Trump's Viral Games force
doctors, janitors, baggers
to become tributes.

April 3, 2020

Early blooms have dropped.
Fresh green leaves replace bare limbs.
Spring marches forward.

Jonquils to tulips—
weeping cherries to lilacs—
spring keeps on springing.

Without our witness,
buds still open, leaves unfurl.
Seasons go viral.

April 4, 2020

Why hoard, save the best
for last? This may be the last.
Better use it up.

Stage 4 tarries not.
In fact, less than two months since
her diagnosis.

COVID upends what
we expect, how we respond
to sickness and death.

Should we go to her?
Should we not? COVID constricts
our human response.

April 5, 2020
Palm Sunday

No palms wave today.
Instead, redbuds dance lightly
during streamed sermons.

Prayers for their pain.
Tears for the lost, the dying.
It starts to hit home.

Tears for the artist.
Tears for the tailor, the dad,
the mamaw, all loved.

Prayers for the doctors,
nurses, those who clean, the kid
who bags bread and milk.

I wish I could thank
them all for what they give to
strangers at the door.

Helpers need much now—
masks, gloves, shields, gowns, meds, supplies—
why can't we keep up?

We need much today—
tests, beds, a machine to breathe,
meds to keep us calm.

We shed, like virus,
to reveal our barest needs.
Each human must breathe.

To our new Clicklist
I add green lightbulbs to mourn
all the lost loved ones.

April 6, 2020

This intersection
of bursting spring/looming deaths
confuses head/heart.

We talk about where
we'll go when bans are lifted,
if we're so lucky.

Our Lenten fasting
includes every part of life—
complete wilderness.

Protect. Shelter. Feed.
Give. Forgive. Help. Heal. Soothe. Breathe.
Love, more than ever.

April 7, 2020

In the next crisis,
I want to be near water,
listening, seeing.

Full Pink Moon rises
as the sun drops, see-sawing
above us down here.

Pink Moon, pinkish sky,
dogwoods, redbuds, tulips. Pink.
The color of love.

John Prine died today.
When I cross the Green River
he'll always be there.

A lifetime crossing
the Green River taught me where
my Paradise lay.

April 8, 2020

Easter is coming.
No matter where we huddle
rebirth can happen.

We hide from COVID.
Wash hands. Pray we don't die. Hope.
Miracles happen.

April 9, 2020
Maundy Thursday

Foot washing, ancient
act of hospitality,
but no guests allowed.

This Maundy Thursday
the concept of Last Supper
feels possible, close.

How do we love now
when we can't touch or visit?
From the heart, always.

How do we love now
while we can't gather or hug?
Find ways from afar.

Loving each other
looks way different this year.
Find ways to wash feet.

April 10, 2020
Good Friday

On this day of death
thousands more will die worldwide.
COVID's not finished.

On Good Friday plant
seed potatoes—resurrect
the earth—think rebirth.

Plant on Good Friday.
My folks showed their love putting
food on the table.

Ashes, death, virus,
PPE, cancer, masks, death.
Dust keeps piling up.

April 11, 2020
Holy Saturday

Day of harrowing
officially arrives but
feels like it's been months.

Today we wait for
the miracle to happen.
More head to their tombs.

April 12, 2020
Easter Day

I roll over as
the light comes, see bare limbs turn
to living color.

Ash trees, thought dying,
resurrect to fresh green buds
beside the dogwoods.

Resurrection comes,
but only after death claims,
the cycle complete.

Two gathered today
in God's name. Sourdough. Port wine.
Communion at home.

Easter—all things new—
we're given yet another
chance to choose rebirth.

What I've Learned in A Pandemic

I've learned to really wash my hands,
not half-assed attempts but deep cleaning
each crevice, bumpy knuckle, age spot.
I've learned to scrub like it will save me.

I've learned not to touch my face or nose,
hug a friend, lean in to hear a whisper,
take someone's hand, fist bump a kid.
I've learned to keep my distance.

I've learned to mix a 1:100 bleach ratio
for relentless wipe downs, still wishing
I could pass the job to someone else.
I've learned cleaning as an act of love.

I've learned I favor the same old jeans
from an overstuffed closet stocked
for another time, another way of life.
I've learned I intend to travel lighter.

I've learned humans can go unwaxed,
unpainted, undyed, and untrimmed,
but hair still needs to be washed.
I've learned to sip tea while I bathe.

I've learned to make do, not make
another trip, accept substitutions,
unfamiliar brands, bruised apples.
I've learned to temper expectations.

I've learned that spring keeps coming.
I miss the woods, but around me I see
trees bud, flowers bloom, birds mate.
I've learned squirrels are urgent nesters.

I've learned to Zoom for family visits,
go to church on Facebook Live,

chat over drinks staring into a screen.
I've learned introverts get lonely, too.

I've learned that snarky posts may be
final testaments chiseled into virtual
stone with no chance to edit or delete.
I've learned to reconsider my legacy.

I've learned to hunt and gather online,
bake bread, make masks, relearn how
to thread a sewing machine bobbin.
I've learned to resuscitate old skills.

I've learned the coronavirus isn't picky.
It finds us—rich, poor, urban, rural—
but it's not colorblind when it attacks.
I've learned it may be American after all.

I've learned about flattened curves,
that being 60+ years makes us targets,
my beloved older siblings even more so.
I've learned life moves so very fast.

I've learned the precious mechanics
of breathing, how ventilators work,
that patients panic like they're drowning.
I've learned rescuers keep them sedated.

I've learned seemingly healthy folks
may be carriers, whether it's a novel virus,
a hateful spirit, a contagious disregard.
I've learned few are immune from fear.

I've learned, as I wait, to look deeper,
examine my own sore spots, hurt places
I'd long hoped had healed but haven't.
I've learned love remains the lasting cure.

Jayne Moore Waldrop is a Kentucky writer and attorney. She's a graduate of the University of Kentucky (B.A., J.D.) and the Murray State University Low-Residency MFA Program in Creative Writing (fiction). She is the author o*f Retracing My Steps* (2019), a finalist in the New Women's Voices Chapbook Contest, and *Pandemic Lent: A Season in Poems* (both from Finishing Line Press). Her linked story collection, *Drowned Town*, will be published in 2021 by University Press of Kentucky. Waldrop's work has appeared in the *Anthology of Appalachian Writers, Still: The Journal, Appalachian Review, New Limestone Review, New Madrid Review,* and other literary journals. Her fiction has been selected as Judge's Choice in the 2016 *Still Journal* Fiction Contest and as finalists for the 2015 Reynolds Price Fiction Prize, the 2016 Tillie Olsen Fiction Award, and 2017 Still Journal Fiction Contest; and her work has been nominated for the Pushcart Prize and the Best of the Net Anthology. A former book columnist for the Louisville *Courier-Journal*, Waldrop lives in Lexington.

www.ingramcontent.com/pod-product-compliance
Lightning Source LLC
LaVergne TN
LVHW051021080826
845145LV00009B/2728

* 9 7 8 1 6 4 6 6 2 4 8 6 7 *